FIVE REASONS FOR SPIRITUAL APATHY

IN TEENS

WHAT PARENTS CAN DO TO HELP

Rob and Amy Rienow

randall house

For RW, Lissy, JD, Laynie, Milly, Ray, and Rush
— with our prayers that you love the
Lord with all your hearts, forever.

Table of Contents

Introduction

"Whatever!"

Have you ever heard this from your son or daughter? Most parents of teens have heard this word a lot. There are other expressions that often follow:

"I really don't care."
"Fine."
"I don't want to talk about it."
"Sure."
"Seriously?"
"This is so lame."

Often these get mixed in with silence, sighing, slouching, and eye rolling. Many of us mastered these techniques when we were teenagers, but now we are on the receiving end.

What is the common thread running through these words and behaviors? Apathy. This word literally means "without feeling" or "without passion." When teens are apathetic, they simply go through the motions of life...disconnected, flat, appearing not to care. Whatever!

> When teens are apathetic, they simply go through the motions of life...

In this book we will specifically focus on the root causes of spiritual apathy in our teens and what we as parents can do to help.

We all understand when our children lack a sense of passion for chores or homework, but what about when they lack passion for the Lord and spiritual things? They show little or no interest in prayer or reading the Bible. Going to church is more like going through the motions. When you try to initiate spiritual conversations, they act annoyed, try to change the subject, or simply glaze over.

Perhaps it was only a few years ago that your child loved church, was eager to pray, and peppered you with their curious and wonderful spiritual questions. Now they seem stuck, flat, and disconnected.

For many Christian parents, as we sense increased apathy in our teenagers, our anxiety rises as well. They are launching soon—with only a few more years, or months of living in our home under our guidance. We can quickly become overwhelmed with fear as we anticipate the possibility of our child heading out into the world without a strong spiritual foundation.

The Spiritual State of Teens Today

The church in the United States is facing a crisis. George Barna's research from 2013 indicates that 59% of twenty-somethings have stopped attending Christian churches, even though they were active at church during their teen years.[1]

> Our children are facing incredible pressures to love the world more than Jesus. These are desperate times!

However, this is not simply a crisis of young adulthood. Many children are struggling in their faith and Christian worldview in their junior high years.[2]

According to the Nehemiah Institute, from 1988 through 2012, high school students' understanding of Christianity and the teaching of the Bible has declined 50 percent. It is important to note that this was a study of students attending Christian high schools![3]

Our children are facing incredible pressures to love the world more than Jesus. These are desperate times!

Realistic Expectations

Some of our parenting problems and frustrations come from completely unrealistic expectations. As our kids move into their preteen and teen years, we expect to see their growth as represented in the following graph:

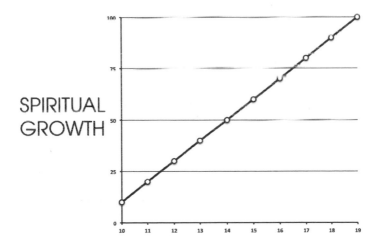

SPIRITUAL GROWTH

Every year, from ages 10 through 19, each son and daughter will become more godly, more mature, more responsible, and more virtuous in every way. This is what we expect. Continual progress. Every week, every month, every year is a step forward. Sounds great, doesn't it?

Think back to your teen years. If you were to graph your development of faith and character, would your graph look like this? Of course, not! No one, at any age, grows or develops in a "straight line."

The Sad Reality

Based on the statistics we looked at above, here may be a more accurate chart on the spiritual growth path for many of our teens today. Things are moving in the wrong direction!

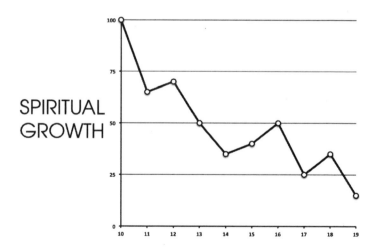

Healthy Spiritual Growth

Here is a picture of what we are looking for. The following graph represents a healthy spiritual track through the teen years.

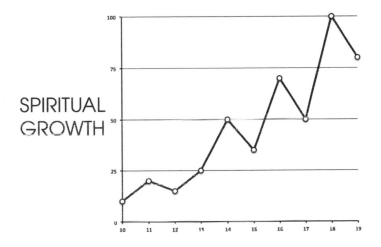

This graph is filled with ups and downs. Some years are filled with progress and maturing. In other years, we lose ground. But look at the trajectory over these 10 years. Taken as a whole, our children are maturing in their faith and their love for God. If the teen years are a continual "two steps forward and one step backwards," that means they are progressing!

Wise parents are realistic. They understand there will be seasons of struggle. However, there is a great danger here. Many parents passively accept the seasons of struggle and apathy in their kids without ramping up their parenting involvement and attention. "He is just 14. He'll grow out of it." "She is just doing what her friends are

> Just because teenage apathy is common doesn't mean it isn't serious.

doing. She'll be fine." Just because teenage apathy is common doesn't mean it isn't serious.

The Spiritual Battle

Take a look at the third graph again—the picture of "healthy" spiritual growth. Look at the "down slope" from age 14 to 15. You can see the same trend from 16 to 17. In this hypothetical example, these are years of intensity, struggle, and spiritual battle. These are periods of time when your son or daughter is under unusual spiritual attack, designed to harden hearts against the Lord and against family.

When our teens are struggling, disconnected, and apathetic, they need our engagement more than they have ever needed it before. This is prime time parenting. Understand that during these time periods, Satan and the demons want to take that "negative trajectory" and drive it all the way down, ending with a spectacular crash of pain, sin, and misery.

Think of a plane that has lost power and is headed for a crash. It is coming down fast and hard. These are the critical moments. Will the pilots and crew do what is necessary to restore power and pull the plane out of its nosedive? Desperate times call for desperate measures. If we have an apathetic child, it is desperate times. It is a dangerous time, where the threat of a massive crash is very real.

When our kids are apathetic, we can easily be tempted to follow their lead and become apathetic ourselves.

> "How many times do we need to talk about this?"
> "Whatever."
> "Do what you want."
> "I'm done."
> "What's the point of talking to you?"

The demons are on the verge of a great victory when apathy and cynicism fills the hearts of both children and their parents.

When you see signs of apathy in your kids, this is your cue to kick into high gear. In these seasons of change, your sons and daughters need your attention, love, parenting, full engagement, and most of all your prayers.

When we first started having children, I thought babies and little kids took a lot of time because they were young and helpless, so parenting them would be easier once they grew older. I could not have been more wrong! Just as the season of childrearing with infants and toddlers is incredibly demanding, so are the teen years. Our adolescents are making decisions that can impact the rest of their lives. They need us more than they have ever needed us before.

The demons are on the verge of a great victory when apathy and cynicism fills the hearts of both children and their parents.

Five Reasons for Spiritual Apathy

If you were to go to your doctor because of a headache, he would ask you a series of questions and examine different parts of your body to determine the cause of your pain. It may be a virus, a bacterium, an injury, or something else. The doctor will consider a variety of potential root causes before recommending treatment.

Just as there are a few basic reasons why someone might have a headache, there are also common explanations why teens struggle with apathy.

Here are five common factors that can cause teenagers to develop an apathetic attitude:

1. The parent's heart is not turned toward the teenager
2. The teenager's heart is not turned toward the parent
3. The presence of secret sin
4. A lack of spiritual nourishment
5. A spirit of rebellion

While these are not the only causes of spiritual indifference, they are common and provide us with a good place to start as we seek to help our sons and daughters grow in faith and character.

These common roots of apathy in teenagers can be used as a series of "check-ups" or conversations to have with your son or daughter when they are struggling. We will give examples of how to do this in the pages ahead.

We join you on this journey, not as parents who have it all figured out, but who are in the thick of raising three teenagers right now (in addition to four younger children).

Our prayer for you is that the Lord will use the Scriptures in this book to equip you to encourage and lead your son or daughter to love Jesus and follow Him forever!

Rob and Amy Rienow

Chapter 1
The Parent's Heart

The first common cause of spiritual apathy we will consider is this: The parent's heart is not turned toward the teenager.

As parents, we are under constant pressure to give our best efforts to our work, friends, hobbies, and even our service in the church. It is easy for our hearts to be "turned" toward these things and for them to become the primary passions of our lives.

Delegation Parenting

We live in a world of delegation parenting. Do you want your children to learn to play the piano? Sign them up for piano lessons. Do you want them to learn basketball? Find a coach. Do you want them to learn math? Hire a tutor. Do you want them to learn about Jesus? Take them to a great youth group. Your job is to simply drive the mini-van and drop your children off with the various experts who will teach and train them for success.

> We live in a world of delegation parenting.

Of course, there is nothing wrong in partnering with teachers, coaches, and tutors as we seek to educate and raise our children. However, when it comes to their spiritual training and the nurturing of their faith, no Christian program can ever replace you! It is so easy for us to slip into the mindset that a youth group or a Christian school is all our kids need to grow in the faith and love for God. However, He has called us as fathers and mothers to be the primary spiritual trainers of our children. Youth groups and Christian education can provide a "spiritual vitamin" boost for our kids, but they were never designed to be a "spiritual meal."

Repentance

Sadly, in the early years of my (Rob's) journey as a parent, my heart was not turned toward my children. Amy and I were married in 1994. During our first 10 years together, I was serving as a youth pastor and we were blessed with four children. Even though I loved my family, my heart was at work. My sense of purpose and calling centered on being a pastor. I was giving my all as a spiritual leader at church, but was spiritually passive at home. I had visions, dreams, and ideas for how I could help all the kids and teens in our church hear the Gospel and learn to follow Jesus…all the kids in the church except for mine. In 2004, God brought me to a deep place of repentance, and He turned my heart to the ministry of my children. He awakened a sense of passion and purpose in me. He had called me as a Christian to "make disciples," and that Great Commission calling needed to begin at home with my own family. My heart, for the first time as a parent, was turned toward the mission of doing

> I was giving my all as a spiritual leader at church, but was spiritually passive at home.

everything in my power to impress the hearts of my children with a love for God.

When I (Amy) was a young mother of four small children, I faced a similar moment of repentance. Through a wonderful sermon a friend had passed on to me, the Holy Spirit convicted me about how I was choosing to spend the time with my kids on a daily basis. While I was working part-time as a therapist and a teacher, I was blessed to have a lot of stay-at-home time with my kids. Sadly, I realized that much of this time was being spent on fun activities with good friends and family, yet very little of my hours were spent teaching spiritual truths. Do you know how many opportunities there are in a given day to gently share the Gospel with a three-year-old? Answer: a lot! Yet you have to take the precious moments to do it. If a mom is consistently more focused on getting her kids to activities, playing with the right friends, socializing with other mothers, attending mom's groups and Bible studies, or constantly cooking and cleaning, she will miss many sweet moments for spiritual connection with her children. I have come to realize over my 17 years of mothering, that what I often considered to be bad days were frequently my children's best days. These were the days of lingering, talking, crying, and laughing together. These were the moments that knit our hearts together.

The Great Commandment

Jesus told us there is one commandment that is more important than any other. It is found in Deuteronomy 6:5-7:

> *You shall love the LORD your God with all your heart and with all your soul and with all your might. And these words that I command you today shall be on your heart. You shall teach them diligently to your children, and shall talk of them when you sit in your house, and when you*

walk by the way, and when you lie down, and when you rise.

This may be a familiar verse to you. Here we find the great purpose of our lives—to be in a love relationship with God, a relationship that brings Him glory. But immediately after God gives us this "great commandment," He speaks to parents and to families. He gives parents a mission: "Teach [My commandments] diligently to your children."

Every Christian has heard the challenge, "You need to share your faith with others. You need to tell people about Jesus. You need to live out the Great Commission." What these words from Deuteronomy 6, and others like it, teach us is that if you are a parent—if God has entrusted the immortal souls of children to your care—then your "Great Commission" begins with them! You are called to share your faith—beginning with your children. You are called to tell people about Jesus —beginning with your children. And remember—your children are your spiritual responsibilities while other ministries are spiritual opportunities. There is a continual temptation to put our opportunities before our responsibilities.

If we want to love God and desire for our children to love Him too, what can we do? Are there any practical steps we can take to lead our children toward Christ? The beginning of verse 7 gives us the starting point: "Talk about [God's words] when you sit at home..." God could not make it any clearer. Mothers and fathers are to take the lead in talking with their children about the Lord and about His Word in the context of the home.

Your children are your spiritual responsibilities while other ministries are spiritual opportunities.

This call to parents immediately follows the most important commandment in the Bible. This is God's call to fully engage our hearts in the spiritual nurture of our children, and that the primary training ground for a child's faith and character is the home.

The Link Between the Testaments

You find this same principle in Malachi 4 and Luke 1. It's interesting that Malachi 4 is the last chapter of the Old Testament, so God spoke these words through the prophet around 400 BC.

> *Behold, I will send you Elijah the prophet before the great and awesome day of the LORD comes. And he will turn the hearts of fathers to their children and the hearts of children to their fathers, lest I come and strike the land with a decree of utter destruction.*

Malachi 4:5-6

Here God ties together the advance of His Kingdom with the "turning of the fathers' hearts" to their children. The mission to build God's Kingdom is a multi-generational mission. This is a serious matter and one that brings with it the threat of judgment.

This is how the Old Testament concludes and it is exactly how the New Testament begins. The next words that God speaks, 400 years later, come from the angel Gabriel when he appears to an old man named Zechariah. The wife of Zechariah was pregnant with the baby who we would later know as John the Baptist. God spoke through the angel regarding John saying,

> The mission to build God's Kingdom is a multi-generational mission.

*And he will turn many of the children of Israel to the
Lord their God, and he will go before him in the spirit and
power of Elijah, to turn the hearts of the fathers to the
children, and the disobedient to the wisdom of the just, to
make ready for the Lord a people prepared.*

Luke 1:16-17

The link between the testaments is the turning of the father's heart to his children! Part of John the Baptist's ministry, in order to prepare the hearts of people for Jesus, was to call fathers to turn their attention, love, and focus to their children.

When the hearts of fathers (and mothers) are fully engaged with their children, and the hearts of children are turned to their parents, everyone's heart is prepared to receive the love of Father God expressed through His Son Jesus. This is why Satan and the demons make it a top priority to harden the hearts of parents toward their children, and children toward their parents; so that everyone's heart will be hard toward Father God.

Our Kids Sense Our Hearts

If our hearts are centered on our work, hobbies, friends, fitness, smartphones, bank accounts, or with whatever game is on TV, our kids will sense it.

It is uncomfortable, but it can help if we regularly revisit questions like these:

- Am I more focused on helping my child be physically healthy or spiritually healthy?
- Do I have more anxiety about my child getting better grades or growing in more godly character?
- Am I spending more energy encouraging my children to keep their rooms clean or to spend time in prayer?

Would your children say, without a shadow of a doubt, that your greatest desire for them is that they love God with all their hearts?

I Grew Up in a Christian Home, But...

In our early years in ministry, we led dozens of youth retreats and mission trips. Often, when we returned from these "spiritual mountain top" experiences, the church would gather for a worship service where students shared testimonies about the trip. So many of the testimonies began like this: "I grew up in a Christian home, but it was not until I went on this trip that God became real to me."

At the time, hearing student after student share these sentiments with the church, we thought it was fantastic. Now, as parents of three teens, we think what it would be like if our children stood in front of a church with a similar testimony. How would we respond if our 17-year-old son, RW, stood in front of the church after returning from a mission trip and said, "I grow up in a Christian home, but it was not until I went on this trip that God became real to me"? Our reaction would be decidedly mixed. On one hand, we would rejoice that the Lord had worked in our son's heart and brought him into a deeper relationship with Jesus. Amen! But at the same time we would be so discouraged. Seventeen years of living in our home, worshiping God together, working through our sins and struggles together, serving together...yet none of these things convinced his heart that God was real and compelled him to want to follow Jesus?

Would your children say, without a shadow of a doubt, that your greatest desire for them is that they love God with all their hearts?

> We never want our faith to be just some sort of lifeless habit—where we go to church because we are supposed to and offer glib prayers before we eat.

We don't know what our children will say when they leave our home. They are not little robots that just do what we tell them or want them to do. But our great desire is that our children would experience the truth and power of God through the daily ups and downs of our family life. We never want our faith to be just some sort of lifeless habit—where we go to church because we are supposed to and offer glib prayers before we eat. What our children experience in our home will impact their hearts and faith for a lifetime.

The Connection to Apathy

Why would a teenager be at risk for spiritual apathy if the heart of his or her parent is not "turned" toward them? If an adolescent has a disconnected parent, it is like the head coach of their team sitting on the bench not offering any direction. There is a leadership vacuum, a lack of guidance, and no encouragement coming from the one who is in the proper position to provide those things. Just as a team becomes lifeless and rudderless when their coach stops coaching, a teen can become indifferent when parents are not engaged in providing spiritual leadership.

Think back to junior high school. We all remember those times when we showed up for class only to discover that our regular teacher was out for the day. There stood the substitute teacher. Everyone knew that while "the sub" might make some attempt to keep us on track, it was party time! We could mentally check out until the real teacher came back. The longer the substitute was with us, the further we fell away from the lesson plan and our progress in the class.

When it comes to your children's spiritual growth, you are the "real teacher." No one can replace you. There is no "sub" that can step in and take the lead on the mission of impressing their hearts with the love for God and encouraging them to grow in faith and character. If you check out, hoping that other substitutes will step in, your child will likely check out, too.

What Parents Can Do to Help

Action Step 1: Honesty

Be honest with yourself about where your heart is turned. Take a moment and pray, asking God to give you insight into your motives and passions. Is your heart turned toward your teenager? Is your heart fully engaged in the mission of helping your son or daughter become a follower of Jesus Christ? Be honest with yourself and with God.

> If you check out, hoping that other substitutes will step in, your child will likely check out, too.

Action Step 2: Confession

To the degree that your heart is not turned toward your child, confess it to the Lord in prayer. "God, I have not been fully engaged in the mission of helping my child know you and love you. I have been overwhelmed and distracted by _____. Thank you that Jesus died for my forgiveness and rose again with the power to change me. Change my heart! Turn my heart to my son/my daughter."

You may also need to confess this to your teenager. "Son/ daughter, God has shown me that I have not been investing my heart and time in the things that matter most. My focus has been more on _____ than on helping you grow in your love for God and His Word. I am sorry. Please forgive me. There is nothing I want more for you than for you to launch into adulthood fully in love with Jesus. I am asking God to help me be a better parent for you."

Action Step 3: Pray a New Course

When God changes our hearts, when He turns our hearts to our kids, things start to change. We do things differently. We start some things, stop some things, change some things, and our conversations begin to change. Why? Because our actions and words always follow our hearts! Prayer is the key to charting a new course and bringing change to our hearts and homes.

The first step on your new course may be taking more time to pray with your teenager, listening to his or her prayer requests, and sharing yours as well. Perhaps you already pray occasionally with your teen, but you don't ever read God's Word together. Reading the Bible together has supernatural power to change your hearts for Christ.

Prayer is the key to charting a new course and bringing change to our hearts and homes.

It may be that your schedule is packed with a lot of "good things," but it is so full that you have little real relationship left with your child. Your relationship has been reduced to saying hello and goodbye as your schedules fly past one another. Maybe your new course begins by saying "no" to some good things so that you can say "yes" to the most important things.

Chapter 2

The Teenager's Heart

A second common reason for spiritual apathy is when the teenager has turned his or her heart away from the parent. In this situation, the parent is engaged and committed to spiritual parenting. The parent's heart is turned toward the child, but the child's heart is not turned back toward the parent. It sometimes seems that the more the parent tries to shepherd and lead, the more the child bristles, rolls his eyes, or hardens his heart.

My Son, Give Me Your Heart

In many chapters in the book of Proverbs, Solomon is writing to his sons. He is writing with life lessons and spiritual instruction. In chapter 23, Solomon makes an unusual request:

> *The father of the righteous will greatly rejoice; he who fathers a wise son will be glad in him. Let your father and mother be glad; let her who bore you rejoice. My son, give me your heart, and let your eyes observe my ways.*
>
> Proverbs 23:24-26

In Christian circles we often talk about "giving your heart to Jesus." We use this phrase to talk about conversion as entering into a personal relationship with Christ. However, the Bible doesn't use that particular phrase in regard to how we are to respond to the Gospel. Jesus doesn't say, "give me your heart" but rather, "Repent and believe" (Mark 1:15). It is here in Proverbs 23 that we find a call to give one's heart; the call is to a child to give his heart to his father.

What does it mean for a child to give his heart to his parent? First, it means the child is open-hearted. He shares his thoughts, feelings, fears, highs, and lows. Second, it means the child has a sense of trust in her parents. As her parents seek to lead her, she knows that they have her best interests at heart, and while she struggles with honor and obedience as every child does, she genuinely wants to be responsive to the discipleship of her parents.

The discipleship process begins as a parent's heart is turned toward the Lord and then turned toward their child. The parent then seeks the child's heart, and the more the child gives his or her heart to the parent, the easier it is for the parent to point the child's heart toward Christ.

Spiritual growth is ultimately centered on the heart. We share our hearts with whoever wins our hearts! This is the priority in the Great Commandment in Deuteronomy 6. Learning and believing the truth of the Bible is essential. Choosing to obey God and do what is right is crucial. But it is possible to

We share our hearts with whoever wins our hearts!

know many of the right things and do many of right things, and still have a heart that is far from God. Parenting is not just hard work, it is heart work.[4]

The Prodigal Path

Over our years in family ministry, we have heard hundreds of personal stories of prodigal children. These were children who, when they were young, seemed to have some signs of spiritual life and health, but now as adults had no visible faith or active walk with the Lord. Every one of these stories is different. However, in nearly every story there was a common experience. The parent of the prodigal shared with us about a time they first sensed their son or daughter "taking their heart away" from them. They started telling lies. They started doing more and more in secret. They increasingly gave one-word answers, especially if the questions had anything to do with God. Personal conversations were off limits.

Have you ever experienced these things with your son or daughter? They clam up, pull back, push you away, and disappear into their private world. This is when our anxiety as parents goes through the roof! The more our children take their hearts away from us, the more fearful we become because we are parenting in the dark. What are they thinking? What are they doing? How are they feeling?

Once this pattern has taken root, we find ourselves reduced to simply managing their behavior. "Make sure you are home at 10 o'clock." "Take out the trash." "Have you done your homework today?" "Did you turn in those papers at school?" All we talk about are the to-do lists, schedules, and getting through each day.

God wants our years of parenting our teens to be far more than schedule management. He wants us to share our hearts with them.

> God's plan is that we increasingly partner with our children in every area of life as we prepare to launch them into adulthood.

He wants our children to share their hearts with us. God's plan is that we increasingly partner with our children in every area of life as we prepare to launch them into adulthood.

What Parents Can Do to Help

If you sense that your child is withdrawing from you, here are some approaches that can help encourage him to turn his heart to you.

Action Step 1: Ask your child to give you his or her heart

This action step is so simple that we often miss it. Follow the example of Proverbs 23:26 and directly ask your child for his or her heart. When we sense one of our children pulling away, becoming uncomfortable with us, or resisting personal conversations, we gently ask for their heart. "Lissy, I have the sense right now that you really don't want to talk with me. Will you give me your heart? Will you let me in and tell me what you are really thinking and feeling?" Sometimes this is all it takes for one of our kids to draw closer to us and talk more openly about a particular situation. Other times the invitation for them to give us their hearts falls on seemingly deaf ears.

Action Step 2: Talk openly about the heart

Another approach sounds like this. "Son, I want to talk with you about something that may be awkward right now, but it is really important. I am sensing that over the last month or two there is something that is not connecting between the two of us. For instance, when I try to have personal conversations with you, or especially religious conversations, it seems that (and I could be way off base) you get a little bristly, annoyed, or uncomfortable. It seems like I get a lot of one word answers and that I am just frustrating you. I then tend to get upset, which makes you upset, and we both go away angry and frustrated. I would love to see this pattern change."

This approach is not meant to "fix" the problem. Instead, it is a warm, slow attempt to soften your hearts toward each other. It is a bumbling, stumbling effort to communicate your awareness that there is a problem and that you genuinely want a healthier connection with your child. Wanting a better relationship with your son or daughter is different than wanting to fix or control their behavior.

If you sense your child's heart becoming cold toward you, don't ignore it! Don't chalk it up to teen hormones. The longer you allow their heart to drift, the longer the journey to retrieve it.

Action Step 3: Ask if you have done something to hurt them

"Daughter, it seems to me that you are a little less comfortable when I am around and I am wondering if I've done something to hurt you. If so, can you please tell me so I can understand and we can talk about it?"

It is a good and godly habit to regularly ask our family members if we have hurt them. Most of the ways we hurt our children is when our anger, harshness, or impatience erupts. When I (Rob) yell at one of our kids, I owe them an apology. It sounds something like this; "JD, I yelled at you. I was wrong. It was not your fault that I yelled at you. I am really sorry I did that, and sorry that I hurt you. Will you please forgive me?"

> Wanting a better relationship with your son or daughter is different than wanting to fix or control their behavior.

If you need to apologize to your children for hurting their feelings through your action or inaction, don't make excuses.

Don't add a "but" at the end of your apology. Just state what you did. Acknowledge you were wrong, sincerely express your regret, and ask for their forgiveness.

In our family, when we apologize to our children, we often finish the apology with the principle from Proverbs 23 and say, "Will you give your heart back to me?"

If we have been harsh and angry with our children, then after we ask for their forgiveness we need to go back and seek to address the original issue in an appropriate way. We may still need to give a consequence for what our child did. The problem is that the first consequence we gave was out of anger. Our harshness did damage to the relationship. Thankfully, we can ask forgiveness and try again.

Action Step 4: Listen more, talk less

Here is a refrain we have heard many times through our years of counseling teens and young adults. "My dad told me the other day that he wants to take me out for breakfast and have a talk with me. What he really means is that he wants me to sit there while he talks. He doesn't really want to talk with me; he just wants me to listen to him talk. He probably has a new list of things I am doing wrong."

The breakfast meeting will happen, but the heart of this teen is already closed off to anything the father is going to say. The walls have already been built.

As our children grow, our parenting style must grow with them. When we have issues with our five-year-old boy, Ray, we do most of the talking. (Although it is always good to listen to our children no matter their age). But if we take this same approach with our teens, we may do more harm than good. Have you ever heard your teen say, "You treat me like I am still a little kid!" They may be right. When we do this to our teens they feel disrespected, and many times rightly so. As our children move through the teen years, we should increasingly relate to them as adults. Sometimes this means a lot more listening and a lot less talking.

Consider asking your teen directly, "Do you feel like I take the time to listen to you and understand your perspective on things? Or do you feel like I am more focused on talking and trying to make you understand my perspective?"

Action Step 5: Affirm honesty

This is an essential ingredient if we want our kids to give us their hearts. They must believe that it is safe to be honest with us, and their belief must be grounded in reality.

One day driving home from church your teen goes on a rant. "Why do we have to go to church all the time? It is so boring. Everyone there is so lame!"

No Christian parent likes hearing these kinds of words. All sorts of emotions rise up within us...fear, sadness, confusion, even anger. We want to "fix it" and make it go away, so we strike back hard. "Young man, we have a great church, and God wants us to be there. It would not be boring if you paid attention! And those people you are calling lame are our friends. They used to be your friends, too. You really need to change your attitude."

> As our children move through the teen years, we should increasingly relate to them as adults. Sometimes this means a lot more listening and a lot less talking.

This knee jerk response is unlikely to yield any positive fruit and will only cause your son to harden his heart even further.

If we are seeking the hearts of our children, the moments when ugly things come out of their mouths need to be handled with the utmost care. So in this situation, instead of pounding him down with correction, we can recognize there was one good thing about what the boy said. He was honest. He was open. It wasn't pretty or nice, but it was honest. He gave you his heart.

So how could we respond differently? First, this is a good time to try and control our emotions, which of course, is easier said than done. You may find yourself pushing back tears or even anger. Pray in your heart, before you speak, asking the Lord for His help. You want to do all you can to communicate to your child that you are pleased, and even proud of him for being honest with you.

"Wow, son, that's a lot. First, I really appreciate you being honest about how you are feeling. You can always be honest with me, whether it is good or bad. How long have you been feeling this way? What else are you feeling about church or the people there? If you could just talk about that for a few minutes, I would appreciate it. I really want to understand where you are coming from."

The goal in this moment is not to fix him. One conversation is not going to do that anyway! The goal in the middle of this conversation is that your son would "give you his heart" and let you in to his most personal thoughts and feelings. This then enables you to compassionately and wisely respond in a way that may help more than it hurts.

If we freak out, panic, yell, or confront, we will do more harm than good.

Perhaps your daughter says, "I am not sure I believe in God anymore." For many Christian parents, just this one sentence would be enough to bring tears to the surface; then we hit the panic button! If we freak out, panic, yell, or confront, we will do more harm than good.

As difficult as it is, we need to retrain ourselves to recognize the silver lining in the situation. She was honest. She opened up. She brought something personal, dark, and difficult to the surface and shared with you. This is a blessing. How terrible it would have been if she was having these thoughts and keeping them secret from you. A teen will share these personal thoughts with those who have her heart, so it is a good sign that she shared them with you.

With this in mind, we could consider this type of response. "Wow, that's a really big statement. First, I am so thankful that you told me. I really appreciate that. I am sure it was not easy to be honest with me because you probably knew it might freak me out…and it does kind of freak me out. But for now, I am just proud of you for being honest. Can you tell me more about what you are thinking and feeling?"

Our purpose here is not to give a script or manual to follow. I (Amy) have found that it is just as important to say, "I am committed to you," as it is to say, "I love you." This is especially true when emotions are going up and down. Our words don't have to be perfect. The goal is to keep imperfect conversations happening.

Again, the aim at this point is not to restore her belief in God. We will focus on that later. Right now, we want to affirm her heart and her honesty. We want her heart! If she will open up and give us her heart with all the details (the good and the bad), the better chance we have to shepherd her heart and point her toward God's great love for her.

Chapter 3

The Presence of Secret Sin

A third common reason for spiritual apathy in teens is the presence of secret sin. Hidden sin acts like a cancerous tumor. It grows and takes over one organ system after another, robbing the body of its strength.

One of the primary symptoms of secret sin is spiritual numbness. We become spiritually flat, disconnected, and apathetic. Sin requires darkness to thrive and grow; it always resists the light. Light and dark cannot occupy the same space at the same time. When we are hiding sin we avoid exposure. We may seek to avoid prayer, Scripture, church, and Christian friends, or only participate passively. A teen may also increasingly withdraw from her parents and family members, especially if her family is seeking to live for Christ.

There are No Secrets with God

We like to think we can keep secrets, but there are no secrets with God.

> For a man's ways are before the eyes of the LORD, and he ponders all his paths.

*The iniquities of the wicked ensnare him, and he is held
fast in the cords of his sin.
He dies for lack of discipline, and because of his great folly
he is led astray.*

Proverbs 5:21-23

Sin looks free and fun, but it is a trap. The more we live in sin, the more we are held fast by its cords of bondage. The demons seek to trick us into thinking we can disobey God in secret, but "a man's ways are before the eyes of the Lord."

Later in Proverbs 9, "foolishness" speaks and says,

Stolen water is sweet, and bread eaten in secret is pleasant.

Proverbs 9:17

Secret sin looks so good! It promises such great pleasure. But the wisdom of God brings truth in the next verse:

*But he does not know that the dead are there, that her
guests are in the depths of Sheol.*

Proverbs 9:18

Sin, selfishness, and secrecy are not the paths to happiness, but ultimately the paths to death.

Pretty Good Kids

Think back to when you were a teenager. Would you say that you were a "pretty good kid?" Many adults use this phrase to describe their childhood and teen years. Sure, we made a lot of mistakes and got into some trouble, but we were "pretty good kids." Right?

> The demons seek to trick us into thinking we can disobey God in secret.

Here is another question. Did you have any dark areas of your life as a teenager?

Were you making choices that were not particularly healthy or good that you kept hidden from your parents?

I (Rob) grew up as a "pretty good kid." I was active in youth group. I was known as a Christian on my school campus. I had a faithful Christian mom. But I had areas of secret sin—inappropriate activity with a girlfriend, attitudes in my heart, bitterness, anger, and more. Perhaps you can relate. The point is even "pretty good kids" struggle with secret sin. "Pretty good kids" keep secrets from their parents.

Just because your son or daughter is a "pretty good kid" doesn't mean they are not struggling with secret sin. If you were dealing with some private things when you were a teen, wouldn't it follow that your teen may be struggling as well?

While there are many areas of secret sin, we would like to address three particularly common ones: sexual sin, drugs and alcohol, and bitterness.

Sexual Sin

With puberty comes a dramatic increase in sexual feelings, thoughts, and drives. For much of human history, when a person was in their mid-teens, they got married and started a family. In today's culture, there is a long gap between the awakening of a person's sexual desires and the godly opportunity to fulfill those desires within marriage.

> Just because your son or daughter is a "pretty good kid" doesn't mean they are not struggling with secret sin.

Our children are bombarded with sexual temptation. Many appropriate websites have banner ads with alluring images. TV shows and commercials have sexually charged content like never before.[5] You can't drive down the highway without seeing billboards with sleaze on them.

Sexual thoughts, lust, masturbation, porn, and sexual activity with boys and girls swirl together in a horrendous whirlwind of temptation for teens today. God created sexuality as a blessing within a monogamous, heterosexual marriage. Therefore, Satan tempts us to use God's gift of sexuality anywhere and everywhere except within God's design for marriage. The world completely rejects the truth that sex is best enjoyed in the context of a committed marriage between one man and one woman.[6]

Not only is there off-the-chart sexual temptation, but also there is equally intense pressure to keep any sexual thoughts, struggles, and activity secret. Sexual sin brings a powerful and unique sense of shame into a teen's life.

God speaks through the apostle Paul describing the powerful nature of sexual sin:

> *Every other sin a person commits is outside the body, but the sexually immoral person sins against his own body.*
> 1 Corinthians 6:18

Sexual sin has a deep and profound affect on a person's life. This is especially true in the teen years when a young man or young woman's sexual identity is forming and their first sexual thoughts and experiences are laying foundations and patterns for their sexuality in the years to come.

Because of the intense temptation in this area, as well as the equally intense pressure to keep sexual sin secret, our children need us to have regular conversations with them about these issues.

For many in our generation, at some point when we were teens, a parent gave us "the talk." That conversation was a one-time event probably lasting less than 30 minutes. It was a rather mechanical explanation of the birds and the bees, and that was it. Some of us didn't even get that much!

Helping our kids develop a healthy sexuality and preparation for marriage doesn't require "a talk" but lots of "talks." Speaking with our teens on a regular basis about issues of sexuality, boys, girls, dating, and romance helps keep these issues in the light and makes the conversations more "normal" and comfortable. Here are questions worth asking:

- How are you dealing with lustful thoughts?
- Are you struggling with fantasizing and thinking about sexual things?
- Are you looking at any pornography? On your phone, on TV, on the web, with friends at school or at their houses?
- Is there anything going on sexually with any guys or girls?
- Are there any guys or girls that you are attracted to right now?
- Are you struggling with masturbation?

> Helping our kids develop a healthy sexuality and preparation for marriage doesn't require "a talk" but lots of "talks."

Sorry to be so graphic here, but these are the real life issues our teens are dealing with, and therefore they need real life conversations with their mom and dad.

> These issues are too important to delegate to the school or youth pastor.

These issues are too important to delegate to the school or youth pastor. We need to take the lead. The world our teens are growing up in is nothing like the world we grew up in when it comes to exposure to sexuality.

Start Sooner

Helping our teens avoid sexually immoral behavior actually should begin when they are young. But it is never too late to make new choices. I (Amy) once heard on a Christian radio station that our culture had lost the freedom to *not* view pornography. If you drive down the highway, you will see provocative billboards. If you watch a sporting event on TV, you will see sexualized commercials. If you walk through the halls in a typical high school, little is left to one's imagination when it comes to scantily clad boys and girls. Listen to the top ten songs on the radio, you will find lust and promiscuity. Suddenly, my eyes were opened to the pornographic world my children were seeing each day. I realized that if I did not say something about all the images they were seeing, I was normalizing this way of viewing the world. We may have lost our freedom to not view pornography, but as a Christian parent I can disciple my children by telling them what is displeasing to a holy God.

From that point on, I made a concentrated effort to open my mouth and tell my kids about the obscenity in our culture and how it stands in opposition to God. For example, when we walked by a well-known lingerie store, I asked them to look away. I said, "I do not want you boys to think it is OK to look at girls like this, and girls I do not want you to think that it is OK for you to dress like that." One time I was trying to get to a children's clothing store at an outside mall. The children's store was only two stores down from this lingerie store. Because I was distracted by my errands, the parking spot I found was directly in front of the lingerie store. Being in my usual hurry, I started to get out of the car, leaving my 14-year-old son in the front seat to watch his siblings while I made a simple purchase return. He lifted his head up and said, "Mom?" Immediately, I got back in the car and moved to a less convenient parking spot. I was praising God that my teenage son was choosing against temptation.

Share Your Story

It may be helpful, as your children grow older, to appropriately share with them the sexual experiences and struggles you had when you were a teenager. Did you make mistakes? Did you do things you later regretted? Appropriately sharing those with your children can be a powerful factor in drawing your hearts together and giving you the opportunity to teach and shepherd them in this area. Knowing that you struggle as well may give them freedom to admit their struggles to you. This is a valuable opportunity to repeat, "You can always tell me the truth. I am here to help you, encourage you, and support you... no matter what."

Ideally, these conversations should be led by the same gender parent. Fathers should take the lead with their sons, and mothers with their daughters. However, this is not always possible. I (Rob) grew up in a home with a single mom and an atheist father. My parents divorced when I was in high school so my mom was the only one there to talk with me about these issues. My dad was not available or capable of having conversations with me about morality and spiritual things. My poor mother was the one who had to talk with me about sexuality, porn, and more. At the time I didn't realize how difficult and awkward this must have been for her. But she did what needed to be done, and I am grateful.[7]

> Knowing that you struggle as well may give them freedom to admit their struggles to you.

Drugs and Alcohol

Just like sexual sin, temptation with drugs and alcohol are very powerful and are usually shrouded in secrecy. In the same way, "pretty good kids" can struggle and become addicted to chemicals.

The pattern is now so common it is cliché. A parent discovers their teen is drinking or using and what do they say? "I had no idea. This totally came out of the blue. I never in a million years would have believed that my son or daughter would ever get caught up in drugs or alcohol." This kind of comment shows how parents are repeatedly blindsided. If we are wise, we will recognize this pattern and take proactive steps not to be taken by surprise.

This may be a good place to give particular attention to our current national crisis of marijuana use. This is a drug that is fairly easy for teens to find, and with its legalization in many states the situation is only getting worse. Users and activists will tell you that pot is no big deal. Nothing could be further from the truth.

The chemical compound in marijuana affects the frontal cortex of the brain and impairs three specific areas of brain function.[8]

First, the chemical in pot turns off "forward thinking." I have to study tonight to pass the test, so I can pass the class, so I can graduate from high school, so I can go to college, so I can get a job. That is forward thinking. It connects my choices today with the results of those choices tomorrow. When people use marijuana, this function of their brain is impaired. Many teens are already struggling with a lack of forward thinking, so imagine what happens when drugs get added to the mix.

Second, weed turns off "impulse control." I really want to do that, but I shouldn't do that, so I won't. Teens who use pot have a reduced ability to resist their impulses. They lose a sense of discipline. They simply do what they want to do, when they want to do it.

Third, pot affects the part of the brain where moral decisions are made. The ability to separate right from wrong is diminished. Everything gets fuzzy.

So teens that smoke pot on a regular basis lose their forward decision making ability, impulse control, and sense of right and wrong. This is why many adolescents that use pot develop a similar type of attitude and personality. All of these effects combine together in a teen's life to create an overwhelming sense of apathy.

Here is another serious reality related to marijuana use—it can take up to a year, after a person stops smoking pot, for their brain to return normal. During this time, it may feel like your son or daughter is a totally different person. In some ways they are. The drug has literally changed their brain and the way they think.[9]

So teens that smoke pot on a regular basis lose their forward decision making ability, impulse control, and sense of right and wrong.

In the same way that we want to be proactive in having regular discipleship conversations about sexual issues, this is an area for repeated and direct discussions. Here are some simple questions to consider asking your children:

- Are there any drugs or alcohol in your life right now?
- Are you facing any temptations to drink or use other drugs?

- · Do you see drugs and alcohol at school or when you are out with friends?
- Are any of your friends struggling with drinking or drugs?

Just because you ask direct questions does not mean you will get honest answers. Keep asking. Keep praying. It may sound strange, but pray for your kids to "get caught." We will never know everything taking place in our kid's lives. We are wise when we tell our friends, "Please tell me if you hear or see anything going on with my children that would concern you. I really want to know." If we don't open that door with other parents and adults who interact with our children, they will be reluctant to share with us. I (Amy) tend to be open with other moms who have asked me to go to that level of friendship with them. However, I will rarely express concerns to a parent who has not opened the door for me to share.

Continue to communicate a spirit of grace and acceptance for your son or daughter, reminding them that no matter what mistakes they make, or what they are struggling with, that you are there to love and support them.

Bitterness, Unforgiveness, and Anger

While there are many secret sins that can cause spiritual apathy in the lives of our children, unforgivenenss is a common one that is often ignored. Does your child hold grudges? Does he continually bring up wrong things people have done? Does she have an "enemies" list, and is it impossible for someone, once they get put on that list, to ever be removed? Does your son seem to go from zero to sixty with his anger? Does it only take a tiny annoyance to cause your daughter to blow her stack?

> Does your child hold grudges?

If you see patterns like these, it may be that your teenager is struggling with the secret sin of unforgiveness. Bitterness can poison your child's friendships, but it is most deadly when it infects family relationships. A child who is struggling with bitterness and anger toward his parents and siblings is in a dangerous spiritual place.

Here is a possible way to gracefully approach the subject with your teen. Let's imagine your son is increasingly bitter and angry toward his sister. "Son, I may be off base on this, but it seems to me that over the past couple of months you have been struggling with anger. I notice your short fuse with your sister and how all she needs to do is look at you funny and you get upset. Again, maybe I am wrong about all this, but could we talk about it?"

Many times, our teens are struggling with a mix of both real and imagined hurts. It can be a slow process to decide which hurts fall into which categories. Of course, your teen will initially believe that all the hurts are real, and none are imagined. There is an important balance here. When our children experience real hurt and rejection, they need our empathy and support. At the same time, if their feelings don't match reality, and we treat imagined wounds as real, we unintentionally shape the hearts of our kids to develop a victim mentality. If your daughter's friend did not text back immediately, it does not automatically mean the friend is shunning her. If two brothers get in a fight, it doesn't mean they hate each other. It is easy to allow small infractions to extrapolate into giant ones. Ask God to give you wisdom to truly empathize with the real hurts your child has experienced and to help them rise above the imagined ones.[10]

It is easy to allow small infractions to extrapolate into giant ones.

The Forgiveness Prayer

If your child opens up to you and acknowledges his struggle with anger and bitterness, ask if he is willing to pray with you. There are two beginning prayers to deal with hurt and anger. The first is a prayer of the will, forgiving the person that has hurt you.

In our example, you might encourage your son to pray like this, "Lord, I am so angry at my sister. I choose to forgive her for what she said to me the other day. I choose to forgive her for being disrespectful to me. I choose to forgive her for making fun of me to her friends." This is the prayer pattern: I choose to forgive (the person's name) for doing (a specific thing).

Here is the second part of a forgiveness prayer. "Lord, I have chosen to forgive my sister but I can't change my heart and my feelings toward her. Please take away any anger, bitterness, and resentment that I have toward her."

This second prayer, where we go to the Lord and ask Him to cleanse our heart of anger, may need to be prayed daily over the course of weeks or even months. I (Rob) faced this in a major way with my father. He had affairs outside his marriage with my mother and my parents divorced when I was 15. I kept praying this prayer for six years before the Lord drained the swamp of my anger and bitterness. "Lord, heal my heart toward my dad. I don't want to be angry with him. I don't want to be bitter." That prayer was lifted up over and over, for six years. God answered it! My anger toward my father was replaced with compassion for him, which enabled me

My anger toward my father was replaced with compassion for him, which enabled me to be a better son and reach out to my father with the Gospel message.

to be a better son and reach out to my father with the Gospel message.

What Parents Can Do to Help

Here is a review of some of the action principles we have talked about in this chapter.

Action Step 1: Invite secrets into the open

It can be helpful to directly ask our children, "Is there any secret sin in your life? Is there anything you are struggling with, that you are hiding, or that you are embarrassed to talk about?"

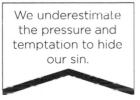

We underestimate the pressure and temptation to hide our sin.

Wrap this question with a spirit of grace and love. You may need to add, "It is OK to be honest with me. I love you no matter what. Dragging secret sin out into the light is the first step toward victory. I want to do everything I can to help you."

We underestimate the pressure and temptation to hide our sin. This goes all the way back to the Garden of Eden. What is the first thing Adam and Eve do after they sin? They run and hide. Sin needs secrecy. It hates the light. Then, after they are confronted by the Lord, rather than take responsibility, Adam starts the blame game.

> *The man said, "The woman whom you gave to be with me, she gave me fruit of the tree, and I ate."*
>
> Genesis 3:12

The woman! It was her fault. You gave her to me! It is Your fault. Eve then proceeds to blame the serpent.

> *Then the* LORD *God said to the woman, "What is this that*
> *you have done?" The woman said, "The serpent deceived*
> *me, and I ate."*

Genesis 3:13

We are all born with this sinful nature, a nature that loves sin and seeks to hide it at all costs. When you see a sinful nature in your son or daughter, remember that they inherited it from you. Humbly invite them to confess to you.

Action Step 2: Share your stories

We all know what it means to sin and to hide our sin. We can appropriately share our stories of failure with our children. This does not encourage them to continue to sin, but to learn from our mistakes and our repentance. When we share our struggles with our growing children, we deepen our relationship with them and we move into a future relationship where our children pray for and encourage us in our faith as much as we pray for them!

Be careful you don't share personal issues with your child to meet your own emotional needs.

Always pray for discernment and wisdom before you share your personal struggles with your child. Be careful you don't share personal issues with your child to meet your own emotional needs. This inverts the parent-child relationship and will result in relational turmoil. Share the things that will benefit your child. Take time to pray before you talk and ask the Holy Spirit to cover your conversation.

Action Step 3: Pray for God to bring secrets into the light

All sinners hide their sin. Your children will struggle with this. Pray specifically for the Lord to bring any secret sins in your child's life out of darkness into the light. Pray for God to give them a sense of conviction over their sin and a spirit of repentance. Pray for God to give them freedom from any bondage they may be in to a particular pattern of sin.

Chapter 4

A Lack of Spiritual Nourishment

Another common reason that teens struggle with apathy is a lack of spiritual nourishment. When children are physically malnourished they lose energy, vitality, passion, and strength. The same is true in the spiritual world. If we are not getting enough spiritual food, we lose our spiritual strength. It may be that your child is spiritually weak because they are not being fed.

Three Square Meals

There are three "spiritual meals" God wants all of His children to have. These spiritual meals are times of prayer and Bible reading. Jesus said,

> *"Man shall not live by bread alone, but by every word that comes from the mouth of God."*
>
> Matthew 4:4b

If we want our children to be spiritually strong, they will need their three spiritual meals. They will need to pray and "eat" God's Word 1) alone as an individual, 2) together with the family, and 3) with the church. Let's talk about each one of these.

Essential Meal #1:
Personal Prayer and Scripture Time

In order for us to be spiritually strong, we need time alone with God. The same is true for your sons and daughters. This is easier said than done. The vast majority of Christians struggle with their "personal devotion" time. It sounds easy to say,

In order for us to be spiritually strong, we need time alone with God.

"Take a few moments each day to talk with God and read your Bible." But it is incredibly difficult. The struggle is not primarily with busyness or distraction, but with spiritual battle. We are in the middle of a holy war, and the forces of evil want to keep us as far away from spending time with God as possible.

In the Old Testament, when God set the Israelites free from their slavery in Egypt, He led them through the wilderness for forty years. Despite their mumbling and grumbling, the Lord provided for them. One of the Lord's miracles was the provision of manna. The people complained that they were hungry, so the Lord made manna, which was like flakes of bread, fall from the sky every day. It was enough to feed them for that day, but they could not store it up or it would spoil. They had to trust God to provide for them each day. It was literally "daily bread." Jesus refers to this miracle when He taught His disciples how to pray, "Give us this day our daily bread" (Matthew 6:11).

In a similar way, we need the bread of God's Word every day. While we can hide God's Word in our heart through memorization, we can have a "fresh meal" every day by taking a few moments to talk with God and read the Bible.

So what can we do to help our children develop the pattern of experiencing this spiritual meal of personal prayer and Bible study?

First, we can ask the Lord to help us set a good example for them. Ask God to help you grow as a man or woman of prayer. Ask Him to give you a greater personal hunger for His Word, so you will spend more time talking with Him and reading the Bible.

Second, we can give our children space in their schedule to spend time with God. Just like we set aside time for them to eat their physical meals, we can set aside time for them to eat their spiritual meals. In our house, we try to include prayer and Bible reading as part of our morning routine. Other times, especially on busy days, one of us will say, "OK, let's all take the next 10 minutes to be alone with the Lord so we can talk with Him and read our Bibles." It isn't easy! Many times we fall short. But with God's help we try again.

We can help our children set aside time to pray and read the Bible. However, what they do with that time is up to them. We can't force our children to pray. Even if we could, it is a bad idea. We can't force them to read the Bible with an open heart. But we can try to model this for them, give them time and space, and warmly encourage them to draw near to God. This is especially true for a teenager who is intensely apathetic about spiritual things.

> We can't force our children to pray. Even if we could, it is a bad idea.

It can be helpful, at a later time in the day, to share with one another what you read or what you prayed about during your devotional time. Avoid legalism here, especially about the time of day for devotions. As a teen, I (Amy) read my Bible before I went to bed. Different times work better for different people. This is about growing in our relationship with God, not setting up a ritual.

Remember, the greatest barrier is spiritual attack. If you go days or weeks at a time without personal prayer and Scripture, confess that to the Lord and ask for His help to begin again.

Essential Meal #2:
Family Worship at Home

In addition to the spiritual meal of personal time in prayer and Scripture, God calls us to "eat" His Word together as a family. Down through the centuries this has been called family worship, or more recently family devotions. Family worship refers to the moments when a family gathers together to pray and read the Bible.

Earlier in the book, we looked at the Great Commandment from Deuteronomy 6. In that passage, God calls us to love Him with all our hearts and then to do all in our power to help our children love Him, too.

> *Love the* LORD *your God with all your heart and with all your soul and with all your might. And these words that I command you today shall be on your heart. You shall teach them diligently to your children.*
>
> Deuteronomy 6:5-7a

In the very next verse, God brings this down into our real practical lives. Do we want to grow in our love for God? Do we want to help our children grow in their love for God? What could we possibly do toward these ends? God answers the question for us.

Talk about [the Word of God] when you sit at home.

Deuteronomy 6:7b

God calls His people to open His book at home with their families. This is the heart of "family worship." Do you want your children to have faith? God says,

Faith comes from hearing, and hearing through the word of Christ.

Romans 10:17

In order for our children to have a strong faith, they need to hear the words of God.

Never Too Late

We often hear parents tell us they were more faithful in praying and reading the Bible

> God calls His people to open His book at home with their families. This is the heart of "family worship."

with their children when they were young, but now that they are teenagers it has fallen by the wayside. Some of this has to do with the increasingly crazy schedule that comes with high school. When our children are young they are physically with us more, which gives us more time for spiritual conversations. In our home, our worship time is always shifting, because our family is always changing.

As a mom of three teenagers, I was lamenting that our family worship and devotional time was not what it used to be.

> In our home, our worship time is always shifting, because our family is always changing.

Every time I made an effort to get our routines back to what they once were, things would fall apart rather quickly. The Holy Spirit gradually began showing me that I needed to stop looking back, embrace my changing family schedule, and adapt

49

to new worship patterns. Because we homeschool, I realized that it was OK for my little ones to stay up later for our family worship time. It may not be every day and these times may not always include everyone. The important thing is that, as a family, we are seeking Him. There are days when we are having "mini" prayer times with different kids throughout the day. We may not always have a consistent pattern of family worship in our home—but praise God we do have a pattern!

Don't Wait Another Day

No matter what family worship has looked like in your household up to today, it is never too late to start—or restart. Years ago, we encouraged a group of adults at our church with this biblical vision for family worship. A mature godly man came to me after the class and said he would try to have a time of prayer and Bible reading that evening with his wife and two teenage daughters. He was feeling awkward and insecure about it so we took some time to pray together before leaving church. It turned out to be a great time for their family. They talked. They prayed. They read the Bible. At the end of their devotion time his 15-year-old daughter said, "Dad, why did you wait so long to do this?" It is never too late.

Based on our surveys in churches around the country, we estimate that only 15 percent of parents today grew up in homes that had a regular time of family prayer and Bible reading. As a result, only 5 percent of church-going families today have a regular time of worship together as a unit at home. Family worship is not parents teaching Bible class to their kids. It is a time when the entire family, with parents in the lead, comes humbly into the presence of God under the authority of His Word. We all need

> "Dad, why did you wait so long to do this?"

the Word of God in our homes, which gives us wisdom, faith, and repentance. Everyone in our household is struggling in the battle against sin and we all need this time of family worship, not just the kids. I (Amy) particularly appreciate when Rob gets on his knees as he leads our family in prayer. For this reason we prefer calling this time "family worship" rather than family devotions.

Starting (or Restarting) Family Worship

The first step for leading big changes in our family is usually confession and repentance. First, humbly tell God in prayer that you have not taken the lead at home in praying and reading God's Word with your family. Receive His mercy and grace through Christ! In addition to confessing to the Lord, you may need to confess this also to your children. Tell them that you feel bad for dropping the ball in an essential area of your parenting. Show them Deuteronomy 6 and the centrality of parents doing all in their power to lead their children spiritually and the importance of families reading the Bible together at home. Ask for your children's forgiveness.

Second, it may be helpful to express your fears and anxieties to your family about trying to start (or restart) your family worship time. "I believe God wants me to help us pray more and read the Bible more together as a family. But honestly, I am really nervous about it. I am not sure how it will go. I don't know how you all will react to it and I am afraid that it will annoy or upset you."

Third, invite your teen's participation in your family worship time. "I think our family worship time will be better if we all contribute our ideas. I wonder if sometimes you could choose a passage from the Bible for us to read? Maybe you could pick a Christian song that you enjoy and we could listen to it together. It would be great to hear why you chose that song and what you like about it."

Fourth, focus on input over output. In other words, the key is the regular honoring of the Word of God as a family. Your teen may or may not participate or respond positively. Don't lose heart. Lovingly share God's Word with him. Faith comes by hearing, and hearing by the Word of God (Romans 10:17).

Family Worship and the Generations

My (Amy's) dear friend Marianne shared the most beautiful story with me about the power of family worship throughout the generations in her family. I have always admired Marianne's consistency as she daily reads the Bible to her boys each morning at breakfast before they go to school. Recently, Marianne has another member of her family daily sitting at her kitchen table in the morning; it is her mother. Sadly, Marianne's mother Ruth is suffering from the early stages of dementia. For the past few weeks, Ruth has been living with Marianne and her family. It was many years ago that Ruth had been the one reading God's Word to Marianne during breakfast. At that time, Marianne had been a disinterested and apathetic teenager in regards to her Christian faith. Her mother kept reading to her. Despite Marianne's foolish heart, the Holy Spirit was working in her life. She would marry a godly man and instruct her children in the Lord just as her parents had brought her up to follow God. Marianne shared with me, "Now my mom is disinterested and she needs me to read the Bible to her at breakfast." What a beautiful story of God's faithfulness throughout the generations of this beloved family.

Your teen may or may not participate or respond positively. Don't lose heart.

Small Steps Forward

The most important thing is to just get started! Add a short Scripture reading at mealtime. Text your teen during the day and ask how you can pray for him or her. Remember that the resistance and anxiety you feel is spiritual attack coming against you. Satan and the demons will do all they can to keep your family away from prayer and Scripture. They can't afford to have the Holy Spirit empower your family with greater faith and godliness. Press in to the spiritual battle. Ask the Lord for help today to take one small step forward.

For additional ideas on how to accelerate family worship in your home, we encourage you to read one of our previous books, *Visionary Parenting* (Randall House, 2009).

> Satan and the demons will do all they can to keep your family away from prayer and Scripture.

Essential Meal #3:
Worship at Church

The third essential spiritual meal every person needs in order to be spiritually strong is worship at church. When the early Christians in the New Testament era met together for their weekly worship service, they gathered with all ages together.[11] This was the practice of Christian churches for the next 1900 years. Unfortunately, during the 20th century, children were increasingly separated from their parents during the church service. While children's ministry and youth ministry can pro-

> When the early Christians in the New Testament era met together for their weekly worship service, they gathered with all ages together.

vide a spiritual boost for kids and teens, they can never replace the church service; the full gathering of the people of God for prayer, worship, and receiving the Word of God.

A Disconnected Generation

Here is the pattern we observe in many churches today. Children grow up through our children's ministries and they love it! They move into the cool middle school group and once again, they love it! Then, it is off to high school with all the events, retreats, and trips. It is a mountaintop experience!

After they graduate high school, these young men and women ask, "Where do I go now?" In many churches the answer is, "You go to church now and get involved with the whole faith community."

I have lost track of the number of high school graduates who have responded, "Well, OK, but I really don't feel that connected with the whole church service thing. Isn't there some kind of college group I can get involved with?"

So what do we do? We whip up a college ministry for them. Four years later when college group is over, they come and ask, "Where do I go now?" We say, "You go to church now and get involved with the whole faith community."

Again the response comes, "Uhhh, I appreciate that and everything, but I don't really connect in that kind of worship. Can we start some kind of new thing on Saturday nights?"

We whip up a new Saturday night "cutting edge" worship service. Then after a couple months or years, they don't come back and ask, "Where do I go now?" They just disappear.

All Together Worship

When a child spends the first 18 years of life being sent somewhere else during the church service, why should we expect them to feel they belong in the church service when they are 19? If we have sought to keep their attention for those 18 years with videos, games, and skits, why does it surprise us that they think "big church" is boring?

The church service is not an adult education hour. It is a gathering of the entire multi-generational community of faith coming into the presence of God. It is a time for all ages to worship Him and to be "spiritually fed" through the worship, prayer, Scripture readings, and preaching. It is a gathering that everyone needs if we are to grow in our faith and remain spiritually strong.

It is a powerful thing to publicly worship God together as a family. When we walk in the doors of the sanctuary together, we don't come in as people who have it all together, but people who need the love and mercy of Jesus. Worshiping together at church enables us to join with Joshua when he declared,

The church service is not an adult education hour.

> But as for me and my house, we will serve the LORD.
>
> Joshua 24:15b

One of the common questions we hear is, "My teen refuses to go to church with us. Should we force him to go?" This is a difficult question for many reasons. First, there is a lot of pain and emotion attached to it—on all sides. Second, because of the unique needs in each family, it is not possible to give a simple blanket statement that appropriately responds to every situation. As a general rule, we encourage you to require your children to attend church with you. As parents, you are the leaders of your family, and you have the right to require things of your children. This should not be done with a heavy-handed approach. We can't force our children to sing, pray, engage with the sermon, or even to be happy about being in church. But we can require them to be there with us and to act in a polite manner. Make your goal regular attendance, not perfect attendance. You don't want to win a specific battle, only to lose the war. If you have an apathetic teen, being with you on a regular basis in a solid, Bible-teaching worship service can play a huge role in softening his heart toward you and the Lord.

> *For the word of God is living and active, sharper than any two-edged sword, piercing to the division of soul and of spirit, of joints and of marrow, and discerning the thoughts and intentions of the heart.*
>
> Hebrews 4:12

Meals and Vitamins

For your teen to be spiritually strong and well-nourished, she will need three square spiritual meals—personal prayer and Scripture time, family worship, and corporate worship at church.

In addition to these three essential meals, there are spiritual "vitamins" that are also available to your children. These spiritual vitamins include Sunday School, youth groups, church retreats, Christian schools, etc. These environments can provide a valuable "boost" for your child. However, vitamins are valuable if they are taken in addition to three square meals. Imagine if you fed your teen nothing but vitamins for breakfast, lunch, and din-

> For your teen to be spiritually strong and well-nourished, she will need three square spiritual meals.

ner! Would your child be nourished or malnourished? Terribly famished indeed! Vitamins alone will not make anyone strong.

Sadly, we have almost two generations in our country that were raised on little more than spiritual vitamins. Parents made it top priority to be sure their children were in Sunday School, youth group, and even Christian schools. While these vitamins can provide a boost, they will never replace the meals of personal prayer and Scripture, family worship, and your church's corporate worship service.

For some families a great way to help their kids get both their meals and vitamins is by making church on Sunday morning a two-hour experience. They worship together as a family for one hour, and the second hour they get their "vitamin boost" in Christian education, youth groups, or adult classes. But we would encourage you to do this—if you are only at church for one hour on Sundays (or Saturday night) that you worship together as a family in the church service. Don't substitute vitamins for the meal.

Don't Give Up!

Helping our teens get these three essential spiritual meals is not easy. It can become increasingly difficult as schedules get crazier or relationships become strained. Don't give up! Your teen may want nothing to do with prayer or Bible reading. Because of their spiritual apathy, they have lost their appetite. If a person is so sick that they are refusing food, you don't cram Thanksgiving dinner down his throat. You nurse him back to health gently; encouraging him to take small bites of good, healthy food. As strength returns, so will his appetite. Take a moment right now and ask the Lord to give your children greater hunger for prayer and Scripture.

Chapter 5

A Spirit of Rebellion

A fifth common reason for spiritual apathy in teens is a rebellious spirit. Some parents make this their first area of focus by making comments such as, "Do you want to know what your problem is? You just have a rebellious attitude!" Often this comes from a heart of anger rather than compassion. Let us encourage you to consider the first four common causes of apathy before jumping to this one.

A Struggling Christian

It is possible for Christians to develop a rebellious attitude. In fact, this is something every Christian struggles with from time to time. It may be the case with your son or daughter. In this situation, you have seen clear evidence of their conversion. There was a time when they responded to the grace of God, were repentant of their sins, and put their faith in Christ to save them. You saw spiritual fruit in their lives, evidence of their salvation, desire for the things of the Lord, and growth in their character. But things are different now. They seem to have gone into spiritual decline. Their thinking is worldly; they are resistant to the things of God, and they are making poor choices. Genuine Christians can, for many reasons, enter periods of their lives where they are not living for the Lord.

Expecting Rebellion

We should expect our Christian kids to struggle with rebellion. When we are born again a struggle begins within us; our old sinful nature fights against the Holy Spirit and our new nature. If someone has never trusted in Christ for salvation, this battle does not exist within them. As we mentioned in the introduction, we should expect our children to face many battles, winning some and losing others. As parents our attitudes toward our children have a significant impact on how our kids will grow in their walk with the Lord. Consider 1 Corinthians 1:4-9 where it states:

> Genuine Christians can, for many reasons, enter periods of their lives where they are not living for the Lord.

> I give thanks to my God always for you because of the grace of God that was given you in Christ Jesus, that in every way you were enriched in him in all speech and all knowledge—even as the testimony about Christ was confirmed among you—so that you are not lacking in any gift, as you wait for the revealing of our Lord Jesus Christ, who will sustain you to the end, guiltless in the day of our Lord Jesus Christ. God is faithful, by whom you were called into the fellowship of his Son, Jesus Christ our Lord.

Take a moment and consider Paul's audience. Paul was writing to a church in the city of Corinth that was filled with "carnal" Christians. This body of believers was struggling with anger, jealousy, divisions, pride, and sexual immorality. It was a church filled with problems and problem makers.

Are your children struggling with sin and rebellion? What is your attitude toward them? Look at the way Paul addresses the Corinthians in the opening of his letter.

Thankfulness

"I give thanks to my God always for you..." Paul begins by expressing his thankfulness for the Corinthians. This is a powerful spiritual principle. Are we giving God thanks for our teens, even when they are deeply struggling? Are we communicating to our kids that we are thankful God gave them to us? When I (Amy) am angry and frustrated with my kids' attitudes and behaviors, thankfulness is not in my thoughts, let alone on my lips. However, when the Holy Spirit convicts me of my ingratitude, I begin thanking God for my children and their struggles. It is powerful for you to tell your child that you are thankful for her, even when she is falling short of your expectations. I am encouraged to follow Paul's example in this letter; to practice thankfulness even when my kids are struggling with rebellion.

Abundance Not Lack

"In every way you were enriched in Him in all speech and all knowledge...so that you are not lacking in any gift." When I read these verses I feel a guilty stamp burned on my forehead! How often am I pointing out to my kids what they lack, as opposed to the abundance they have in Christ? I have a laser-like focus on everything they need to improve: their attitude, their orderliness, their temper, and their language...the list goes on. In Corinthians, Paul addresses believers who are having problems yet he is specifically pointing out all they have in Christ;

not all they are lacking. As parents, this is a great example to follow. Reminding our kids they are "not lacking in any gift" will encourage them. These words of Paul to the carnal Corinthians remind me of Toby Mac's song, "Speak Life" where he prompts believers to:

> *Lift your head a little higher*
> *Spread the love like fire*
> *Hope will fall like rain*
> *When you speak life*
> *With the words you say*

When Christian kids are rebelling, let's remind them of the abundance they have in Christ.

Christ's Faithfulness

"...Who will sustain you to the end, guiltless in the day of our Lord Jesus Christ. God is faithful..." Paul does not place any confidence in the believers at Corinth. Instead, he places all his confidence in the faithfulness of Jesus Christ. He seems to have no doubt that God will sustain them, and he uses this amazing word, "guiltless." Praise God that because of what Jesus has done for us, we as believers will all one day stand guiltless before His throne. Our hope does not rest in our teen's good behavior, but rather in Jesus Christ's determination to draw them back and sustain them. Our hopes and prayers rest on Jesus working in their lives. Paul's emphasis on God's faithfulness to a church full of problems encourages us to trust in His faithfulness when we are having problems with our teenagers.

> Our hope does not rest in our teen's good behavior, but rather in Jesus Christ's determination to draw them back and sustain them.

New Creations in Christ

When the Lord saves us, He does not fix our former broken and sinful nature. Our "old nature" is crucified with Christ. He doesn't revive us, He kills us! He does this because we don't need to be repaired; we need to be reborn. We need to be recreated; we need to be brought from death to life.

> *I have been crucified with Christ. It is no longer I who live, but Christ who lives in me. And the life I now live in the flesh I live by faith in the Son of God, who loved me and gave Himself for me.*
>
> Galatians 2:20

> *But God, being rich in mercy, because of the great love with which he loved us, even when we were dead in our trespasses, made us alive together with Christ—by grace you have been saved—and raised us up with him and seated us with him in the heavenly places in Christ Jesus.*
>
> Ephesians 2:4-6

> *Therefore, if anyone is in Christ, he is a new creation. The old has passed away; behold the new has come.*
>
> 2 Corinthians 5:17

It is possible, however, that as new creatures in Christ, we choose to live like the old, dead, sinful person we used to be. We are no longer slaves to sin because we are now free in Christ, but we are voluntarily acting once again like slaves.

The Apostle Paul himself struggled with this.

> *For I do not understand my own actions. For I do not do what I want, but I do the very thing I hate.*
>
> Romans 7:15

> *For I do not do the good I want, but the evil I do not want*
> *is what I keep on doing.*
>
> Romans 7:19

Grace and Truth

If you believe that your son or daughter is born again, but is struggling with their old sin nature, your ministry to them must be filled with grace and truth.

God spoke through the Apostle John telling us about the person and work of Jesus:

> *And the Word became flesh and dwelt among us, and*
> *we have seen his glory, glory as of the only Son from the*
> *Father, full of grace and truth...For the law was given*
> *through Moses; grace and truth came through Jesus*
> *Christ.*
>
> John 1:14, 17

Jesus came full of grace and truth. This should be our prayer goal as parents; that we would minister to and shepherd our children, full of grace and truth.

Grace

Most of us are better at one than the other. Some parents are filled with grace. They communicate their love and acceptance clearly and regularly. They frequently respond to crisis with gentleness, not wanting to push their children away.

My (Rob) father was heavy on the grace side. Even though he was an atheist and hard-hearted toward God, he tried to communicate love to me. He said this to me many times, "Bobby if you rob a bank, I will still love you." When I was

> Jesus came full of grace and truth.

a kid, I thought that was quite strange for him to say. But as I grew older I understood what my dad was trying to say—that even if I made mistakes, he would still love me. I am grateful for the grace and acceptance my dad gave me during my formative years at home.

Truth

Other parents are more naturally inclined toward the ministry of truth. "Son, I am concerned about your behavior." "Daughter, the choices you are making are wrong, and they are going to lead to misery for you." "Son, I need to be blunt with you and tell you that what you are doing is against the will of God." Honest truth!

If you read through the New Testament, you will see that Jesus was full of grace and truth. His "volume dial" on grace was cranked up to 10. His "volume dial" on truth was also cranked up to 10. One never watered down the other.

Full Volume!

Here is an exercise to help you crank up the volume on grace and truth. Take out a piece of paper and draw a line down the center. On the top left, write "full of grace," on the top right, "full of truth." On the left side of the page write a series of sentences that communicate "full grace" to your son or daughter. Ask yourself, "What would be the most gracious and loving things I could possibly say to my children as they are going through this difficult time? How can I best communicate my unconditional love and unconditional commitment for them?" Here are some possibilities:

> His "volume dial" on grace was cranked up to 10. His "volume dial" on truth was also cranked up to 10. One never watered down the other.

- I will always love you.
- There is nothing you can do that will make me love you any less.
- There is nothing you can do that will make me love you any more.
- I am completely committed to you.
- When you do wrong things, I still love you.
- I will always be there for you, no matter what.

The key ingredient on the "full of grace" side of the page is, "I love you."

> The key ingredient on the "full of grace" side of the page is, "I love you."

Now turn your attention to the right side. What do you need to say that would communicate "full truth" to your teen? Truth expresses honest concern. Truth confronts sin. Truth tells it like it is.

- I am concerned about the choices you are making.
- I am concerned about the lack of spiritual interest in your life.
- The path you're on is not the path of godliness.
- I am concerned that you are going against what God says in the Bible.
- I am concerned that you are damaging important relationships in your life through the choices you are making.

The key ingredient on the "full of truth" side is, "I am concerned." Sometimes sin needs to be called sin. Sometimes a rebellious attitude needs to be called out and named. If we turn up the truth volume, without turning up the grace volume, it will certainly

> The key ingredient on the "full of truth" side is, "I am concerned."

do more harm than good. When we speak truth to our children, it must be wrapped in a genuine pleading of our heart for them to turn to the Lord and follow Him.

Consider Jesus' call to us, full of grace and truth:

> *"The time is fulfilled, and the kingdom of God is at hand; repent and believe in the gospel."*
>
> Mark 1:15

> *"Whoever has my commandments and keeps them, he it is who loves me. And he who loves me will be loved by my Father, and I will love him and manifest myself to him."*
>
> John 14:21

> *"For God so loved the world, that he gave his only Son, that whoever believes in him should not perish but have eternal life. For God did not send his Son into the world to condemn the world, but in order that the world might be saved through him. Whoever believes in him is not condemned, but whoever does not believe is condemned already, because he has not believed in the name of the only Son of God.*
>
> John 3:16-18

> *"Those whom I love, I reprove and discipline, so be zealous and repent. Behold, I stand at the door and knock. If anyone hears my voice and opens the door, I will come in to him and eat with him, and he with me."*
>
> Revelation 3:19-20

Do we love our children enough to plead with them to follow the Lord when they are living for themselves? Do we love them enough to tell them the truth when they seem to be living for the praise of man rather than the praise of God? Do

> Do we love our children enough to plead with them to follow the Lord when they are living for themselves?

we love them enough to tell them the truth when the choices they are making are sinful? When "full truth" is wrapped in "full grace" we follow Christ's example and give our children a blessed opportunity to repent and be restored in their relationship with us and with the Lord.

What If My Teen Is Not Saved?

It may be that your son or daughter has a rebellious spirit because they are not born again. They are still in the same state in which they were born—which is spiritually dead. As a result, they are acting, thinking, and feeling like a dead person. They may have been brought up in a Christian home and Christian church, but that does not automatically make one a Christian. It may seem harsh to say these things. No one likes to think of children, especially our own, as "spiritually dead." Yet, this is the reality of our sinful nature.

> *And you were dead in the trespasses and sins in which you once walked, following the course of this world, following the prince of the power of the air, the spirit that is now at work in the sons of disobedience—among whom we all once lived in the passions of our flesh, carrying out the desires of the body and the mind, and were by nature children of wrath, like the rest of mankind.*
>
> Ephesians 2:1-3

Unfair Expectations

We are zero for seven on getting kids "with virtue" from the factory. Maybe God missed our kids on the days He was putting kindness, joy, and obedience into the new babies. All of our children have come into the world "wired up" to lie, disobey, hit, and steal. Sin is their natural state and inclination.

One of the things we do with our kids when they are young is to expect virtue and character out of them that they simply don't have. I (Rob) expect my kids, for example, five-year-old Ray, to be happy, pleasant, joyful, giving, and not apt to throwing my remotes in the trash. However, my expectations are not met with this child or any of my others! They naturally lie, bite, kick, and steal...all of them! From whom could they possibly have inherited all that stuff?

> We are zero for seven on getting kids "with virtue" from the factory.

Despite the fact that our children are not born with virtue "built in," we expect them to live virtuously. How unfair. How can we expect goodness out of someone who is spiritually dead? Children don't need to be taught the right rules and then forced to obey. They need to be forgiven of their sins and born again.

Here is one of the most common questions we hear at our Visionary Parenting seminars. "The consequences I give my kids have stopped working. Do you have any creative consequences that will change my kid's behavior?" There are no consequences that can give your children virtue. Consequences only tap down bad behavior. Our children need to be spiritually transformed by God.

> There are no consequences that can give your children virtue.

A Call for Compassion

If you become increasingly convinced that the root issue behind your son or daughter's spiritual apathy is their lack of spiritual life in Christ, we hope you are overwhelmed with compassion. This was Jesus' attitude when He saw the lost multitudes.

> *When he saw the crowds, he had compassion for them, because they were harassed and helpless, like sheep without a shepherd.*

> Matthew 9:36

If our children are dead in their sins, apart from Christ, they are, spiritually speaking, harassed and helpless, like sheep without a shepherd. We have known some parents who, in a fit of anger, have yelled, "I wonder if you are even a Christian!" This is perhaps the most unhelpful thing we can possibly say. If we believe our children are apart from Christ, our hearts should break, not burn with anger. We should also be overwhelmed with a sense of urgency for their salvation.

I Just Can't Be Good

A number of years ago our daughter Lissy was habitually being harsh with her younger sister. Day after day, we talked about it and tried to give her consequences. Nothing changed. More talking. More consequences. Finally, after a few weeks of this, Lissy became so frustrated that she blurted out, "I just can't be good!" This was not a flippant comment. It came from a deep place in her heart.

> If we believe our children are apart from Christ, our hearts should break, not burn with anger.

How would you respond if your son or daughter said this to you? Our instinctive response might be to say, "Oh, honey, sure you can! It will be all right. You are a good girl. You just need to try harder. You can be good. I know you can."

In that moment, God helped us with what Lissy really needed to hear. "Lissy, you are so right. You can't be good. Do you know why? Because the Bible says you were born with a bad nature. I am not saying that to be mean or to hurt your feelings. It is just the truth. We were born with a bad nature, too! So you are right, you can't be good. But there is great news. God loves you! God has made a way for you to be forgiven for all the badness in your heart. Jesus is proof of God's love for you. Jesus is God's Son, and God put all your sin and all my sin on Jesus, and when He died on the cross He died to pay the price for our sins. Jesus did not stay dead, but came back to life three days later—winning the battle over death and sin. Jesus takes our badness and gives us His goodness. When this happens, God changes our hearts. We tell God we are sorry for our sins, and we put our faith in Jesus to save us. Jesus promises to keep changing our hearts, making us more and more like Him. In Heaven, Jesus will finish His work and we will never sin again."

The Gospel and the Power of God

If you are concerned that your son or daughter has not been born again, look for opportunities to share the full Gospel with them. What do we mean by the "full Gospel?" The word "Gospel" means "good news." And indeed, the message of the Bible is good news! But the message does not start with good news. The message is not simply, "Jesus loves you." Before we get to the wonderful love of Jesus, there is bad news…news none of us want to hear.

The bad news is that we are sinners. Why do we keep doing things wrong, and thinking things even worse? Why is the world filled with violence, abuse, stealing, and corruption? It is all our fault. It is all because of our sin…our wicked hearts and wicked actions.

> *…for all have sinned and fall short of the glory of God,*
>
> Romans 3:23

> *They have all turned aside; together they have become corrupt; there is none who does good, not even one.*
>
> Psalm 14:3

And here is the part our sinful natures hates—there is nothing we can do to save ourselves. There is nothing we can do to earn points with God. No amount of so-called good deeds can cover up or outweigh our sin. Many wrongly believe that at the final judgment God will take the good from our life and put it on one side of the scale, and the bad on the other side. Whichever way it tips is Heaven or Hell. This is not true. The fair penalty for even one sin is death.

> There is nothing we can do to earn points with God. No amount of so-called good deeds can cover up or outweigh our sin.

> *For the wages of sin is death…*
>
> Romans 6:23a

We hate this message because of our pride. We want to believe that we are good enough to make God like us. We want to believe that if we try hard enough we can make it to Heaven. We want to believe that our good intentions and our will power can make us better.

> *…God opposes the proud…*
>
> James 4:6

The Good News begins with terrible news. We are sinners doomed to hell and there is nothing we can do to save ourselves.

What Must We Do to Be Saved?

If there is nothing we can do, how can we possibly be saved? Can we be forgiven? Can our dark hearts be made right? Now we get to the Good News!

Now we get to the Good News!

For while we were still weak, at the right time Christ died for the ungodly. For one will scarcely die for a righteous person—though perhaps for a good person one would dare even to die—but God shows his love for us in that while we were still sinners, Christ died for us.

Romans 5:6-8

For the wages of sin is death, but the free gift of God is eternal life in Christ Jesus our Lord.

Romans 6:23

But he was pierced for our transgressions; he was crushed for our iniquities; upon him was the chastisement that brought us peace, and with his wounds we are healed. All we like sheep have gone astray; we have turned—every one—to his own way; and the LORD has laid on him the iniquity of us all.

Isaiah 53:5-6

It is often said that we are not saved by works, but this is not exactly true. We are not saved by our works. We are saved by the work that Jesus did on our behalf—taking our sin, taking the wrath of God, dying in our place, and conquering sin and death through His resurrection. It is this work, the work of Jesus, that makes it possible for us to be forgiven and saved.

> We are saved by the work that Jesus did on our behalf—taking our sin, taking the wrath of God, dying in our place, and conquering sin and death through His resurrection.

Repent and Believe

How should we respond to this Good News? Jesus tells us in His very first recorded sermon. God calls us to repent and believe!

The time is fulfilled, and the kingdom of God is at hand; repent and believe in the gospel.

Mark 1:15

…If you confess with your mouth that Jesus is Lord and believe in your heart that God raised him from the dead, you will be saved.

Romans 10:9

But what God foretold by the mouth of all the prophets, that his Christ would suffer, he thus fulfilled. Repent therefore, and turn back, that your sins may be blotted out, that times of refreshing may come from the presence of the Lord, and that he may send the Christ appointed for you, Jesus.

Acts 3:18-20

But these are written so that you may believe that Jesus is the Christ, the Son of God, and that by believing you may have life in his name.

John 20:31

Repentance is a radical change of mind. We change our mind about ourselves. In our sinful nature we believe we are naturally good and our sin is no big deal. When we repent, we acknowledge our sin and our need for a savior.

To believe in Jesus is to put your faith in Him, to trust Him to save you. It is a turning from faith in yourself to faith in Christ. It is trusting that Jesus truly died on the cross and rose from the dead, and

> Repentance is a radical change of mind.

that is your only hope of salvation when you stand before God on judgment day.

> For by grace you have been saved through faith. And this is not your own doing; it is the gift of God, not a result of works, so that no one may boast.
>
> Ephesians 2:8-9

This message—the bad news of our sin, the good news of Jesus' love, death, and resurrection, and the call to repent and believe—this one and only Gospel is the power of God unto salvation (Romans 1:16).

Pleading Through Tears

Have you ever been so burdened for the souls of your children that you were brought to tears? This was the case for the Apostle Paul, not with his own children, but with the young Christians he was teaching. Acts 20:31 tells us he would plead with people, through tears, to trust Christ, follow Him, and believe His Word. Do we have this same passion as parents,

> Have you ever been so burdened for the souls of your children that you were brought to tears?

or do we sometimes share the spiritual apathy we see in our teens?

This is not about manufacturing artificial emotion, but having our hearts match up with reality. If the reality is that one of our own children is not following Jesus, it is only right that our hearts should be burdened, and that burden should accelerate our desire to point our children to Christ.

Only God Can Change the Heart

You are reading this book because you see a lack of spiritual passion in your child's heart. Changing the heart of a child is the work of God, and He often chooses mothers and fathers as His primary instrument. There is no quick fix for heart change. There is no 1-2-3 parenting magic. We begin with humbling ourselves before the Lord and asking Him to work a miracle of grace and mercy in our hearts and the hearts of our children.

In the final chapter, we have suggested a series of prayers based on Scripture, which seek to address each of the five common causes of spiritual apathy.

Chapter 6

Heart Changing Prayers

Only God can change our hearts, and the hearts of our children. Therefore, our most significant work as parents is in prayer. Here are a series of prayers, based on God's Word, which may help you as you respond to the five common reasons for spiritual apathy.

Prayers for the Parent's Heart

Lord, please help me to love You with all my heart, all my soul, and all my strength. Place your commandments on my heart. Use me to impress the hearts of my children with a love for You. Enable me to make our home a place of prayer, Scripture, and worship. (Paraphrased from Deuteronomy 6:5-7)

God, give me a greater passion to lead my children to know and love You. Raise up the next generation of this family with an even greater love for You! Bless my children so greatly that they will then in turn share the good news of Jesus with our grandchildren, great grandchildren, and beyond. (Paraphrased from Psalm 78:5-7)

Prayers for the Teenager's Heart

Lord, please work a miracle in the hearts of my children. Cause them to grow more and more with a love for You, with knowledge, and with wisdom. Make them pure, filled with the fruit of righteousness that comes through Jesus Christ. (Paraphrased from Philippians 1:9-10)

God, turn my child's heart to You and to Your truth. Unite our entire family with one faith in your Son Jesus Christ. Please show my child your grace, mercy, and peace. (Paraphrased from 2 John 1:1-3)

Prayers Against Secret Sins

Lord, bring to light the things now hidden in darkness. Bring any secret and sinful thing in my child's life into the light, with a spirit of confession and humility, so he can experience your grace and forgiveness. Through this process, use me as an instrument of love. (Paraphrased from 1 Corinthians 4:5)

God, set my teenager free from any bondage to secret sin. Bring her into the light, and deliver her from darkness. Remind her that the blood of Jesus cleanses us from all sin. Do not let her be deceived, but give her the grace to confess her sins and be cleansed from all unrighteousness. (Paraphrased from 1 John 5:7-9)

Prayers For Spiritual Nourishment

Lord, give my son a desire to pray to You and to read Your Word. Help him to store up Your Word in his heart, and not sin against you. Give him a true love for the Bible and for talking with You in prayer. (Paraphrased from Psalm 119:8-16)

God, help our family grow in family worship. Help us talk about Your Word when we sit at home, when we walk along the road, when we get up, and when we lie down. Let us always be able to say, "As for me and my house, we will serve the Lord." (Paraphrased from Deuteronomy 6:5-7 and Joshua 24:15b)

Dear Lord, unite our family in our worship at church. Bring all our generations together, with our brothers and sisters in Christ, with a true desire to worship You. Guard us against the spiritual attacks that would cause us to put other things before church. From an early age, help our children eagerly look forward to worshiping You each Sunday. (Paraphrased from Psalm 102:12, Psalm 146:10, Hebrews 10:24-25, and Nehemiah 12:43)

Prayers for Salvation

Lord, work a miracle in the hearts of my children and bring them to repentance of their sin and faith in Christ. Fill them with the Holy Spirit. Make them new creations in Christ, and use them to make a difference in this world for You and Your Kingdom. (Paraphrased from Acts 2:38-39 and Ephesians 2:10)

God, show Your mercy to my son. Show him the seriousness of his sin, and that he cannot do anything to overcome it. Bring him to truly repent and trust Christ for his salvation. Bring my son out of death into life, out of the darkness into light. (Paraphrased from Ephesians 2:1-9)

A Final Prayer of Blessing

Finally, would you join us in lifting up this prayer of blessing for our children?

May the LORD bless and keep our children;
May the LORD make His face to shine upon them and be gracious to them;
May the LORD lift up His countenance upon them and give them peace.
Amen. (Paraphrased from Numbers 6:24-26)

Endnotes

[1] Three Spiritual Journeys of Millenials, https://www.barna.org/barna-update/teens-nextgen/612-three-spiritual-journeys-of-millennials#.VXhdFkIeXwx.

[2] Ken Ham, *Already Gone: Why Your Kids Will Quit Church and What You Can Do to Stop It* (Master: Green Forest, AK, 2009).

[3] This research from the Nehemiah Institute is explained in graph form here: http://www.nehemiahinstitute.com/index.php.

[4] Scott Turansky, *Parenting Is Heart Work* (David C Cook: Colorado Springs, CO, 2005).

[5] Jeanette Mulvey, "Why Sex Sells More Than Ever," June 7, 2012, http://www.businessnewsdaily.com/2649-sex-sells-more.html.

[6] Glen T. Stanton, "Male Sexual Satisfaction and Marital Longevity," February 5, 2013, http://media.focusonthefamily.com/fotf/pdf/fof_daily_broadcast/2013/ffde-20130117-research-about-sexual-satisfaction-in-marriage.pdf.

[7] Here are two suggested resources that may help you as you have honest and helpful conversations with your teen about sexuality:
-Passport2Purity Getaway Kit from www.FamilyLife.com
-Barrett Johnson, *The Talks*, (INFO For Families, 2014).

[8] Three important studies on the effects of marijuana on brain function:
-http://consumer.healthday.com/public-health-information-30/marijuana-news-759/brain-scan-study-suggests-pothead-stereotype-might-be-real-683062.html.

-http://health.usnews.com/health-news/news/articles/ 2013/07/02/brain-scans-suggest-marijuana-may-squelch-motivation.

-http://www.ncbi.nlm.nih.gov/pubmed/21145211.

[9] Another study related to long term brain impact from pot use:

-http://www.amenclinics.com/blog/marijuana-causes-long-term-brain-changes/.

[10] As you help your children with hurt and anger, here are two resources that may help you:

-Lou Priolo, *The Heart of Anger*, (Calvary Press: Amityville, NY, 1998).

-Neil Anderson, *The Bondage Breaker*, (Harvest House Publishers: Eugene, OR, 2006).

[11] Acts 20:7-12, Ephesians 6:1-13, Colossians 3:20.

FAMILY.

It's at the very heart
of the global cause of Christ.

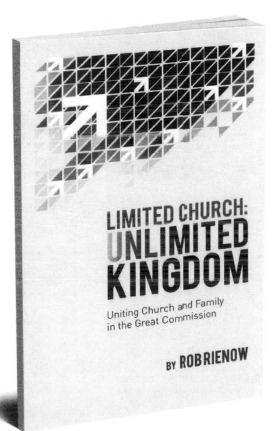

LIMITED CHURCH:
UNLIMITED
KINGDOM

Uniting Church and Family
in the Great Commission

BY ROB RIENOW

EVERY
MARRIAGE
MATTERS
TO GOD.

After years of counseling engaged and married couples, the Rienows realized that most Christian couples didn't know why God had brought them together! *Visionary Marriage* will reveal that God does have a plan and a purpose for marriage and family in the Bible. The focus is on the big-picture purpose for marriage, and the goal of successfully understanding that purpose.

Ideal for small group study with discussion questions at the end of each chapter.

Visionary Marriage by Rob and Amy Rienow $12.99
Group discounts available

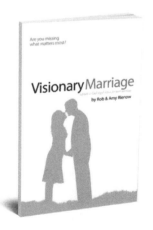

D6family.com   800.877.7030

What is **D6**?

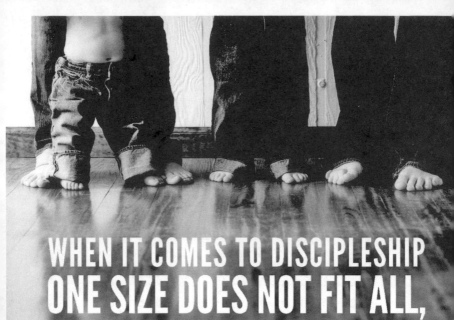

DISCOVER
IMAGINE
PURSUE

↗ What is God calling you to do?
↗ How does He want you to do it?

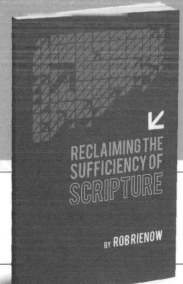

RECLAIMING THE
SUFFICIENCY OF
SCRIPTURE

BY ROB RIENOW

FROM AUTHOR
ROB RIENOW